MY LITTLE BOOK OF
BIG MONEY

SIMPLE FINANCIAL TIPS
FOR A WORRY-FREE FUTURE

PAUL A TRAN

BEAVER'S POND
PRESS

Edited by Ashley Brooks and Abbie Phelps
Illustrated by Bob Lipski
Book design and typesetting by Dan Pitts

ISBN 13: 978-1-64343-565-7
Library of Congress Catalog Number: 2024906362
Printed in the United States of America
First Edition: 2024
28 27 26 25 24   5 4 3 2 1

BEAVER'S POND PRESS

Beaver's Pond Press
939 Seventh Street West
Saint Paul, MN 55102
(952) 829-8818
www.BeaversPondPress.com

To order, visit www.patranwrites.com. Reseller discounts available.

Contact Paul A. Tran at www.patranwrites.com for school visits, speaking engagements, book club discussions, freelance writing projects, and interviews.

A FOOL AND HIS MONEY ARE SOON PARTED.

—Attributed to Thomas Tusser

To my beautiful wife, Nikki—
every "I" throughout this book
should be interpreted as "we"
since you're my other half.

CONTENTS

INTRODUCTION

DISCLAIMERS

To start things off, I want to point out that this book has to do with financial concepts and laws that are specifically applicable in the United States. If you don't live in the US, some of the topics in this book might not be relevant to you.

Also of note: *I'm not a financial advisor.* I don't want you to think that I am. I'm just a regular guy who's good at math and who loves planning for his own financial future. This book isn't meant to provide financial advice to you specifically; it's simply how I view my own finances and an attempt to communicate what I've learned and what's worked for me. It's what I wish I'd known earlier, and I hope it launches you on a path to your own financial freedom—if you aren't already well on your way.

Long story short, if you read this book, you agree to not sue me.

A MESSAGE FROM THE AUTHOR

I remember when I got my first "real" job after graduating college and received my first "real" paycheck. I analyzed every line on it. I saw that some of it went to taxes and the stuff that I was used to seeing from my previous (lower-paying) jobs. There was something new, though. *What is this "401(k) deduction" I see?* I googled it and never looked back. I still can't believe I had never learned about a 401(k)—or retirement planning in general—until that point in my life. Ever since, I've spent more time than I'm comfortable saying reading about the intricacies of financial planning and planning for retirement.

What's in this book might not be the "perfect" way to do certain things, so I encourage you to look into everything I say. Fact-check me. Let me know if you find an error or think that I got something wrong. Maybe there are better alternatives in some situations. Look at the current retirement outlook for most Americans, however, and it becomes clear that things aren't pretty. Feel free to skip the next section if you want to just believe me when I say the retirement outlook is ugly—like, really ugly. But if you've been neglecting your finances for too long, you probably know already.

A recent report from the Federal Reserve reveals the following:[1]

- Forty-four percent of non-retired adults don't think their retirement savings are on track.

- Twenty-five percent of non-retirees have no retirement savings of any kind. Zero. Zilch.

- "One-third of people in their [thirties] who had some self-directed retirement savings, but less than $50,000 worth, felt that they were on track." If you're in your thirties and have less than $50,000 saved, then you almost certainly are not on track. We'll cover this later.

- Fifty-two percent of adults with a credit card carried a balance on their credit card month over month in the past year—and, therefore, are almost certainly paying outrageous interest rates.

- Sixteen percent of adults simply aren't able to pay their bills.

- Twenty-eight percent of adults couldn't pay their bills if faced with an unexpected $400 emergency expense.

---

1 Board of Governors of the Federal Reserve system, "Report on the Economic Well-Being of U.S. Households in 2019, Featuring Supplemental Data from April 2020," May 2020, https://www.federalreserve.gov/publications/files/2019-report-economic-well-being-us-households-202005.pdf.

These are only some statistics provided by a single report. There are countless other surveys and reports that paint a similarly dire picture. For example·

- According to a survey done by Bankrate, 22 percent of Americans have no emergency savings at all.[2]

- The median retirement savings among all adults is about $65,000.[3]

- According to the Federal Reserve, the median retirement savings of Americans between ages fifty-five and sixty-four (or retirement age) is $107,000.[4] Most people probably couldn't survive on this amount of money for five years. If they were to retire, they might have to try to stretch that amount for forty or more years.

To summarize, the majority of Americans are truly lost when it comes to handling their financial situation. That's why I'm writing this book. I hope it teaches you something by simplifying complex financial topics, encourages

---

2 Lane Gillespie, "Bankrate's 2023 Annual Emergency Savings Report," Bankrate, June 22, 2023, https://www.bankrate.com/banking/savings/emergency-savings-report.

3 Amelia Josephson, "Average Retirement Savings: How Do You Compare?" Smartasset, last modified August 7, 2023, https://smartasset.com/retirement/average-retirement-savings-are-you-normal.

4 U.S. Government Accountability Office, "The Nation's Retirement System: A Comprehensive Re-Evaluation Is Needed to Better Promote Future Retirement Security," GAO, October 2017, https://www.gao.gov/assets/gao-18-111sp.pdf.

you to become more confident with your finances, and helps you take a step in the right direction for your financial future.

Now, regarding what you're about to read: I've had many casual conversations about personal finance with friends, family, and coworkers. I tried to write this book as if I were talking with them. I tried to capture how I think about my own finances. I separated this book into short lessons because, well, I'm lazy (we'll get to that in a minute). I don't like reading long chapters. I often find myself dozing off, not recalling what I just read, rereading the same section, giving up, and placing the bookmark halfway through the chapter, only to read the entire chapter again the next day. That's why I broke this book down into short sections. I prefer to get to the point quickly and efficiently without wasting time. So, if you find yourself getting bored and losing focus, don't worry about putting the book down. You won't have to catch yourself up later. Actually, if you find yourself losing focus, *please do put the book down and come back to it when you're focused.*

CHAPTER 1:

COMMON CENTS

YOU'RE LAZY!

I'm lazy. I've always been lazy. I'm fine with admitting it. It's who I am. I yearn for a time when I can wake up at noon on a Tuesday, go play a round of golf (I don't play golf, by the way, but if I had time, I'd like to try it), take my dog for a walk, and do whatever else I feel like doing for the rest of the day, all without having to worry about money.

In fact, I'm so lazy that I work myself to the bone. My desire to be lazy has driven me to do things that I didn't realize I was capable of. It's caused me to accomplish things I wouldn't have dreamed I could do even a few years ago. I've delivered papers, pushed carts, bagged groceries, stocked shelves, served tables, sold electronics, and cleaned up feces and vomit, and I hated it. My bed is so warm. The sky is so blue. Why do I have to go into work? My desire to do whatever I want has pushed me every step of the way. It pushed me to get a degree in computer engineering and follow it up with earning my master's degree in engineering management. It was the best investment I saw for my future at the time. And I think that's how people should think of their lives: continuously making **little** investments that will make a **big** difference in their futures.

While in college, I almost always had the best grade in the class. You'd often find me getting kicked out of the engineering lab when it was closing at 2:00 a.m. and find me waiting when it opened back up at 7:00 a.m. This wasn't because I loved school but because *I absolutely hated school*. I wanted to make sure there was no possibility that I'd ever have to take that same course a second time. If I graduated and couldn't find a job, God forbid—I'd have to do it all over again. I hated college because, you guessed it, I'm lazy.

After college, I've continued to educate myself and have worked for some of the best companies in the world. But if you told me I could sleep in and play video games in my pajamas instead of going into work (and there would be no work to catch up with the next day), I'd do it in a heartbeat.

One important thing to keep in mind: Being lazy doesn't just have to motivate you to work *harder*. It should also motivate you to work *smarter* in your current situation.

OVERSPENDING

I grew up poor. I know how much it sucks. It blows my mind that some people will never experience the struggles of being poor. They will never know what it's like to have your (extremely strong and proud) mother pull you aside on Christmas, begin to cry, and apologize because your Santa is broke and couldn't afford the remote-control car you wanted. They don't know what it feels like to be an eight-year-old placing pots and pans on the floor to catch the water from your leaking roof, watching your mother cry into her hands because she doesn't know how to fix it.

We weren't poor due to a lack of income. My parents actually had a modest income. We were poor due to poor financial decisions.

My mother could (and did) live on next to nothing while raising five kids. On top of that, she also constantly

had to chase her husband around, as he spent money as if there were no end to it.

I'll give credit to my dad; he was extremely driven. He still is. He came to America with literally nothing but the clothes on his back and a younger brother to take care of. When he arrived here, he worked on a farm for less than minimum wage, somehow worked his way through college, and eventually was able to become the lead electrical engineer overseeing an entire manufacturing facility at a Fortune 500 company. He faced racism, never questioned authority, and spent money that he didn't have. He dreamed of winning it big and worked hard to make decent money, but he was awful with the money he was already earning.

I'm slowly realizing that I was able to witness a great lesson firsthand. I was able to watch someone who was incredible with money while she stayed married to her polar opposite.

My father gambled away at least $55,000 that I know of—at least, that was the amount I know he put on hidden credit cards. My mother eventually found out, and it quickly became her problem to solve.

This would likely be a crippling amount of debt for someone today, so you can imagine what it was like in the early nineties for someone raising five children. I remember my mother saying, "In two years, the credit cards will be paid off if we keep paying them at this rate." This was after she'd already spent years paying toward the cards. I remember seeing the hope and excitement she had at the prospect of no longer being shackled by credit card debt.

To say that being poor sucks is an extreme understatement. It's humiliating. It's hopeless. I wouldn't wish it on my worst enemy. That said, I was lucky enough to see firsthand what makes someone poor. A few poor decisions lead to a few worse decisions. I witnessed how fear, worry, and anxiety can hold you back from earning more.

I witnessed how uncontrolled spending doesn't give you a chance to get your head above water.

A PENNY SAVED IS A PENNY EARNED

From a financial perspective, I treat my life as if it were a business. And any successful business is very familiar with *net profit*. To calculate net profit, subtract expenses from your income.

INCOME – EXPENSES = NET PROFIT

For most of us, this can probably be calculated by simply looking at our checking account. How much did you earn this month? How much did you spend? Net profit is so important that your bank statement likely summarizes your income and expenses each and every month already. Feel free to go take a look.

I remember a time my mother and I were walking to her car and caught sight of a penny. Even as a seven- or eight-year-old, I didn't bother with it—but she reached down and proclaimed, "A penny saved is a penny earned!" If you look at the net profit equation, you can see what the saying really means. Decreasing a penny of expense is the same as increasing your income by a penny; either way, your net profit went up by a penny! However, I don't entirely agree with the saying, because a penny saved is

actually worth significantly *more* than a penny earned; you've already paid taxes on the penny you save, whereas the government wants a cut of the penny you're earning.

If you're reading this book, you're likely searching for ways to increase your net profit. Looking back at the equation, you can see that there are only two ways to do this: increase your income or decrease your spending. Let's start by talking about how to reduce spending and bad debt.

CHAPTER 2:

ELIMINATE SPENDING AND BAD DEBT

BAD DEBT

The first thing that needs to be addressed is bad debt. For the sake of this book, I'll define *bad debt* as unnecessary expenses that don't increase your income (and, therefore, decrease your net profit). Credit card debt, excessive loans, high phone and cable bills, bank overdraft charges, ATM fees, late fees; eating at high-end restaurants, buying luxury accessories and expensive electronics. You know what I'm talking about. Bad debt. These are often things you can do without that also charge you high interest rates, lose value quickly (depreciate), or simply waste your hard-earned money.

CREDIT CARDS

The average individual American had $6,365 in credit card debt in 2023.[5] Any credit card debt that you're being charged interest on is too much credit card debt. Yes,

---

5 Chris Horymski, "Experian Q2 2023 Consumer Credit Review," Experian, October 24, 2023, https://www.experian.com/blogs/ask-experian/consumer-credit-review/.

I understand that some people have accrued their credit card debt paying for necessities: hospital bills, groceries to feed your family after a job loss, or other *emergencies*. I don't have any problem with that. When I was in college, I injured myself, couldn't work, had no savings, and had to survive for a few months on credit cards alone. That said, I did everything I could to (1) minimize my spending and (2) pay off my debt as quickly as possible once I could work again. What I would consider to be *bad debt* is when people buy things that they don't really *need* and then don't or can't pay off those credit cards in full every month. Then they continue putting small amounts of additional debt on those same credit cards and are never able to pay them off.

How much will you have paid to that credit card company once you're done making ten or more years of minimum payments at 20 percent interest? Too. Damn. Much. That is, of course, if you don't continue to put more on credit cards while you're making minimum payments. Then you'll be paying even more.

As an example, let's pretend you're married, and you and your spouse each have roughly the average amount of credit card debt—so a total of about $12,000. Let's also pretend this debt has an interest rate of 20 percent and that you're making minimum monthly payments of $240. You'll have the debt paid off in just over nine years. But you'll also have paid about $14,000 in interest during this time. Think about that. You'll pay more than twice what you actually spent simply because you spent the money before you had it. Those $200 headphones that you don't really *need* will actually cost you about $433. If you consistently do this with all your purchases, then everything you buy costs over double what it should. Do you see how this can easily spiral out of control?

Now, let's pretend you always have $12,000 on credit cards. What I mean is that each month, you make a payment of $240, but you also spend a little more on the credit card. Since the interest comes out to be about $200 per month at 20 percent interest, you'll only need to spend about $40 per month on that credit card to *never* pay it down. In other words, you're paying $240 to spend $40 (paying six times what you actually spent!) and enjoy a never-ending supply of stress because you owe $12,000 in credit card debt. Those $200 headphones are actually costing you $1,200. Would you still buy those headphones knowing that?

Over those same nine years, you will have paid $21,600 in interest alone. If you didn't have this debt, you could have saved this money and ended up with $21,600 sitting in your bank account at the end of nine years. Or, you could have invested this money into something that *would earn you more money*, resulting in significantly more than the $21,600 saved. Or, you could do literally anything else with it—simply donate it to a charity you believe in, give it to your parents, buy a car with cash, you name it. I think we all can agree that just about anything would be better than donating that money to the credit card companies.

Credit card interest is bad debt, and it should be at the top of your priority list to get rid of, since there are few things in life with higher interest rates. You should take it personally that you're donating your hard-earned money to your credit card companies. When I talk about debt throughout this book, I'll be referring to bad debt. Yes, there is "good debt," or debt that increases your overall net profit—we'll talk more about that later. But when most people refer to *debt*, they really are talking about *bad debt*.

Not only does debt cost you monetarily (likely in the form of more debt), but it also places extreme stress on you and your loved ones—and understandably so. Sleepless nights, not being able to focus, depression, fear, your overall happiness . . . these are the things that often accompany bad debt.

The moral of the story is that if you do use a credit card, you had better be paying it off *in full* every month. If you can't do that, you should do everything in your power to not use credit cards *at all*—or you might find yourself paying six times over for every purchase you make.

Now that your credit cards are paid in full every month (or maybe even more often than that), it's all right to not use them at all. However, I personally take full advantage of credit cards. I pay them off in full and haven't been charged interest on a credit card in about 20 years. If you're going to use them, my suggestion is to find one that gives you as much cash back as possible. There are a few out there that give 2 percent back without any annual fees (I hate fees, if you haven't noticed). The key here is that you can't think of a credit card as something you can pay off at a later date. You need to think of a credit card as something you pay off *today* (or tomorrow when it goes through, I suppose). You should consider that money spent from your bank account as soon as you charge that card. That money is no longer yours—you spent it. And you should transfer the money to pay it off as soon as possible to make sure that your bank account knows it.

If you don't have the money in your bank account, then you shouldn't be charging to that credit card! I pay off my credit cards multiple times per month (I do forget sometimes if I'm busy at work, but I never go more than a couple of weeks). I also have my credit cards set up to automatically pay off the statement balance at the end of the month as backup—and make sure I have plenty in my bank account to cover it. By paying credit cards off often, having them set up to pay the statement balance off every month, and ensuring I have enough in my bank before charging to that credit card, I've essentially guaranteed that I will never pay interest to a credit card company.

GETTING RID OF BAD DEBT

So that's bad debt—but how can you get rid of it? The easiest thing to do would be to prevent the debt in the first place, of course. Don't buy those $200 headphones. Get rid of your cable TV altogether. Stop (or at least reduce) going out to expensive restaurants. Create a budget and *stick to it*. As for the debt you've already accumulated, there are two main strategies of paying these down that I think are worth mentioning: the Debt Snowball and the Debt Avalanche. Before we dive into these, however, I'll point out the obvious: if you're getting rid of the debt you already have, then you should not be adding additional debt on top of it. As previously described, that would make the situation much worse.

THE DEBT SNOWBALL

The Debt Snowball is for those of us who need gratification sooner rather than later. Think of it as a tiny snowball (your surplus payment amount) rolling down a snowy hill, starting small and growing larger and larger with each debt it knocks out. Overall, it won't save you quite as much money as paying off your debt with the highest interest rate first, but it will save you more than not paying down your debt at all. And that's what most people with debt struggle with: continuing to stay on course to paying off the debt. People give in to the urge to spend money on things that temporarily make them happy. I get it. I do it sometimes too. But we need to do whatever it takes to stay motivated and continue to make progress. That's where the Debt Snowball succeeds.

Here's how the Debt Snowball works: you write down your debts in order of how much you owe. You then pay the minimum payment on all your debts *except for the smallest debt*. This small debt is the one you will focus all of your attention toward. It's the one debt you want to get rid of as quickly as possible. You should apply any and all extra payments toward this small debt until it's paid off. It should be paid off relatively quickly, and once it's paid off, you should take the money that previously would have gone to paying that debt and apply it to the next-smallest debt. Again, once paid off, focus on the next-smallest debt and so on, until even the largest debt is now manageable and freedom is in sight. Each of these debts, as they're paid off, should give you some gratification, additional cash flow (the money you no longer owe), and motivation to continue paying down additional debt.

By the time that Debt Snowball has knocked out all your debt, you'll now have a huge snowball of money each month to do something else with. Remember, the snowball represents the surplus money you were putting toward your debt. Without debt, that giant snowball doesn't have to knock out any more debt. It all goes into your pocket!

THE DEBT AVALANCHE

The next strategy, the Debt Avalanche method, is simple—and it's my personal favorite. If you stick to it, it will pay off your debt the quickest, saving you the most money in the end. The strategy is simple: Again, you write down your debts, but this time, you sort them by their interest rates, from highest to lowest. You then make minimum payments to all your debts except for the one with the highest interest rate. Again, this debt is the one you will focus all your attention toward. It's the debt that you want to get rid of as quickly as possible. Once this debt is out of the picture, it will free up additional cash flow, which will allow you to focus on the next debt with the highest interest rate, and so on, until all your debt is paid off. The main difference here is that by paying off the debt with the highest interest rate first, you are reducing the negative effects these debts have on your expenses.

Don't take my word for it, though. There are several online calculators that will cater to your specific debt, show you how much the avalanche method will save you over the snowball method, and perform a few other neat tricks. Go ahead and google "snowball vs. avalanche calculator," enter your debts, and take a minute to research it for yourself.

GOOD DEBT

There's also good debt. I'd define *good debt* as any debts or expenses that have a strong likelihood of increasing your net profit, either by increasing your income, decreasing your expenses, or both.

Suppose that you invest in solar panels that cost you $10,000 up front but reduce your electric bill by an average of $100/month forever. After a decade or so, you'd come out ahead, and this would increase your overall net profit. However, good debt isn't always guaranteed, and it can quickly become bad debt. Maybe you take out a small business loan to start up that business you've always dreamed of. If that business thrives and dramatically increases your income, this would obviously be good debt.

If the business fails and you have to close up shop, you'll now be left with a loan but no chance of earning money on this investment. You'd quickly change your mind about that debt and consider it bad debt. As an aside, this exact situation happened to me, and I don't regret it. I opened a brick-and-mortar business that ultimately failed, and I only recently paid off the loan. I predict this won't be the last time it happens to me, either. You have to risk money to make money sometimes.

Mortgages

An often-debated debt is a home mortgage. If no one will let you live rent-free in their basement, you most likely will have to pay to live somewhere, either by paying someone rent or by taking out a mortgage. A mortgage is not without risk, however. If you purchased your first home in 2007 before the housing market crash, you likely would not consider that mortgage to be a great investment in 2011. However, if you purchased in 2011, you likely *would* consider your mortgage to be an incredible investment in 2021.

Despite these market fluctuations, one constant of having a mortgage is that it will definitely save your rent payment (which is money you would never see again). Instead, you'll be making payments toward your home. Assuming you take out a fifteen- or thirty-year fixed-rate mortgage, you'll own the home outright in that many years.

Take my situation as an example. I rented throughout college at the cheapest possible places I could find. I was in a college town, and rent was cheap. After college, I moved to a suburb of the city, and rent prices were roughly double what they were in my college town. Instead of renting, I opted to purchase a home in the country that was a *short sale*—a home that is being sold for less than what the previous owners owed on its mortgage. The monthly mortgage payment was less than if I had rented. I was lucky; the housing market significantly increased, and this turned out to be a great investment. After about six years, I was offered a job in the city, and living in the country was no longer an option. I sold the home for almost double what we had paid for it. We took some money and invested it, then put a decent amount toward our next (and current) home only a few miles from downtown. This house cost roughly three times what our original house had. Since then, the housing market has continued to increase, and our house is now worth about twice as much as what we currently owe, even without making any extra payments.

Again, none of this was guaranteed, but it was a risk I was willing to take—home prices increase faster than inflation on average, meaning the odds were in my favor to come out ahead. Overall, the equity I have in my home now is easily more than I've paid in mortgage payments since I purchased that first house. If I had rented instead, I would have paid in about the same, but I would have nothing in equity today.

Also, take note: the median home price in 2023 is about 70 percent more than it was even in 2007, so those who held on to their property until 2023 rather than selling after the market crashed are likely pretty happy with their decision. This is also a good overall investment lesson, as we can see similar patterns in the stock market throughout history (and will almost certainly continue to see this in the future).

Education

An education, whether it's to become a neurosurgeon or an electrician, is, in my opinion, the perfect example of good debt. It is an investment like any other investment. It's an investment of your time as well as your money. This is the perspective I took when I considered going to college. I knew I would be spending a significant amount of time going to school—time I could have spent working at a company and gaining experience, getting raises, being promoted, and so on. It would also be spending a significant amount of my money. I wasn't the brightest kid, so I hardly pursued scholarships at all and paid for college almost purely out of my own pocket. When I considered college, I had to figure out if it was really worth it or not. I analyzed the investment using the net profit equation I previously mentioned:

INCOME – EXPENSES = NET PROFIT

Again, I remembered my parents and how their situations differed. My mother didn't finish college and had a tough time finding work that was nearly minimum wage. My father, on the other hand, pursued an electrical engineering degree and never had an issue finding work. His salary paid over triple what my mother earned. Taking this into account, I considered the cost of going to college. I tried to minimize my expenses as much as possible by estimating the cost of spending my first two years at a community college followed by two years at a relatively cheap accredited university. I estimated that the total cost for a bachelor's degree in computer engineering would be roughly $30,000—not including lost income from not joining the workforce and gaining experience. I then took into account the pay difference between getting the degree and not getting the degree. At the time, as I recall, the median software developer earned about $95,000 a year. Without a degree, the median income was less than $40,000 annually. Simply taking that into account, it was obviously going to be a very good investment. I likely wouldn't have to struggle to find work and would see a pay increase of about $55,000 in annual salary.

I understand that colleges and universities are increasing their rates much faster than inflation, so by the time you're reading this, it might not seem like a great investment to go to college. I'd argue that it's tough to put a price on knowledge, however, and it might be something you would regret not doing when you look back on life. An education will increase your earning potential, help push you to think in ways you might not have otherwise, and allow you to get jobs that are out of reach without an education. Because of this, the cost of an education would have to be astronomical before I'd ever recommend against it.

To be clear, an *education* should not be confused with a *college experience*. These two concepts are not mutually exclusive, however. If you're planning to go to college for the *experience* and not for the *education*, it almost certainly will not be a good financial investment, and I would recommend against it—if not for your personal finances, then out of respect for the university, the trade school, and/or the other students who are prioritizing their *education*.

Choosing a major or area of focus is equally important when you think about your financial future. I don't want to put down some degrees or areas of focus, but factually speaking, some fields simply don't earn as much on average as others. Some degrees aren't as marketable, so you'll have a tougher time finding work. This is why I chose to pursue a bachelor's degree in computer engineering. I researched majors as if it were my job. I made the decision because it left me with quite a few options. I learned electrical engineering as well as software engineering. This meant that I could become an electrical engineer, hardware engineer, software engineer, software developer, programmer, and so on. I checked the Bureau of Labor Statistics website (BLS.gov) as well as many other sources and saw that, at the time, all these occupations paid well and had very low unemployment rates. The software-focused occupations' job outlooks were projected to grow significantly, which helped to predict demand (and how difficult it would be for me to get a job).

To put it bluntly, this simply isn't true for many areas of focus, so I highly suggest doing this same analysis for the major you might be considering. Look at the current unemployment rate. Look at the job outlook. Look at the number of people graduating in the field. Look at the median salary you might expect after graduating. Then make an educated decision on whether it's the right major for you.

SAVINGS MINDSET STRATEGIES

It's tough to avoid bad debt if you don't have a strong savings mindset. Decreasing expenses increases your overall net profit and savings potential. Not spending money can be tough, though—we need to find motivation to help us out. When tempted to splurge, there are several easy ways to remind yourself of your savings goals.

Hours Worked

Instead of thinking of money as dollars and cents (or simply a magic credit card), convert the money you're thinking of spending into hours worked (after tax, of course). To illustrate, assume you take home $1,600 (after tax) over the course of two weeks. You really want that new phone that just came out (even though your phone works great and can do everything you *need* it to do). Let's say that the new phone costs $800. Is that phone really worth a full week of work? Is it worth . . .

- Getting out of your warm bed in the morning while your alarm clock screams at you?

- Having to pick out clothes while you're half-asleep?

- Driving through thirty minutes of stop-and-go traffic each way?

- Stressing out about that late project?

- Whatever else you don't like about work?

Now do that all over again the next *four days*—all for a phone that is adding little or no value to your life. That phone may open an app slightly faster than your current device or have some cool feature that you'll use twice and forget about—was it worth that entire week of work? Probably not. Skip that new phone, and you just saved yourself a week of work.

Cash Only

Another technique is to simply use cash. As my wife's grandpa says, "Five bucks here. Five bucks there. Pretty soon, you don't have any beans!" Swiping a credit card doesn't evoke the same emotion as handing over your hard-earned cash. Half the time, you probably don't even know how much you spent until you check your receipt or credit card statement. Seeing the money leave your hand might not prevent you from purchasing whatever it is you're purchasing right there and then, but it might remind you of how much you spent earlier in the day or earlier in the week—and therefore, prevent you from spending more later on. This is a proven way to decrease spending.

Create a Budget

The goal of budgeting is to keep your spending in check. Most of us know roughly how much we'll earn week to week or month to month, so we can create a budget of how we'll spend that money. The tighter we can be with our budget, the less our expenses will be, and the more net profit we'll have to save and invest. If you're using the cash method, a very popular way to do this is to simply put cash into a different envelope for each category you spend your money on, such as groceries, clothes, gas, and so on. When you want to check how much you have left to spend in that category, just count the cash left in the envelope. If using credit or debit cards, you'll have to either manually keep track of your budgeted categories or download an app to help you with them (this is what I do). The nice thing about apps is that many let you tie all (or most) of your accounts to them so you can see all of your finances at a glance, rather than having to log in to each account individually.

Wait It Out

Wait until the next day or week before you buy something. My wife and I have a rule that we never buy anything "expensive" without reviewing it with each other first. Our threshold for "expensive" is $200, which might be more or less than what you would deem to be expensive. To be fair, we usually review smaller purchases with each other as well.

We also never buy anything expensive on the spot. If you find yourself with a pushy car dealer, you might end up buying a car that you really don't *need*—or even want. It's easy to get out of the situation, though—just tell them, "I have a strict rule that I never buy anything on the spot. I'll need to think about it." Then do just that. Take a week to think about it. The more impact the purchase has on your net profit, the more time you should take to think about it.

REDUCING TEMPTATION FURTHER / PAYING YOURSELF FIRST

If you have money burning a hole in your pocket, then you shouldn't let that money get to your pocket in the first place. Avoid having excess money in your bank account, and instead funnel it automatically into savings that are hard to get at. For example, if your company offers you a 401(k), put as much toward that as you can afford. This way, you'll never even see the money, as it automatically gets taken directly out of your paycheck and saved for "future you." If your 401(k) is maxed out, put money toward your individual retirement account (IRA). If that's maxed out, then maybe a health savings account (HSA) makes sense for you.

(Note that this is oversimplified, and possibly not even the right order of accounts you should be investing in. The main point here is that you should invest as much as you

can afford into retirement vessels like these. We'll also talk more about all these options later in the book.)

You can also automate saving and investing to your brokerage account (which is just an account that lets you buy things like stocks) or somewhere else you don't look at often—thereby reducing the temptation to cash out and spend that money. I strongly suggest automating investments as much as possible. You could automate a "payment" to be pulled from your bank account and placed into your brokerage account the day after payday. Think of it as a *bill* that you *must pay*. To illustrate, my house payment comes out the day after I'm paid every month. On the same day, I've also automated an additional payment to my brokerage account. I always make sure I have enough in my bank account to cover both "bills."

CHAPTER 3:

EARN FREE MONEY

We're now on our way to driving down our expenses and are looking for ways to increase our income (and net profit!). My favorite way to increase income is to do as little as possible because, well, I'm lazy. This chapter will cover a few ways to take advantage of . . . *free money*!

FREE MONEY!!!
PART ONE: 401(K) MATCH

If someone walked up to you and handed you a check for $100,000, would you take it? You'd probably think it was too good to be true. What if it were true, though? Of course you would take it—it's free money! Or say your employer wanted to give you a raise of 6 percent. Would you turn it down? Of course you wouldn't.

There are people out there *who do* turn this free money down, though—millions and millions of people, actually. They say, "No thank you, my dearest employer. You keep that money. I'd prefer to work for less." Yes, I said "employer"—employees are turning down free money. The worst

part about it? Those employees probably don't even realize the horrible mistake they've made until it's too late!

If you haven't guessed what I'm talking about yet, it's a company's 401(k) match—or 403(b) match, or whatever retirement vessel your line of work has. Since a 401(k) is the most common, I'll refer to these as 401(k) plans throughout the rest of this book. According to the US Census Bureau,[6] 79 percent of workers have access to a

---

6 Maurie Backman, "Does the Average American Have a 401(k)?," Motley Fool, last modified June 19, 2017, https://www.fool.com/retirement/2017/06/19/does-the-average-american-have-a-401k.aspx.

401(k). However, only 41 percent of those who have access are actually taking advantage of their 401(k). According to the US Bureau of Labor Statistics,[7] 51 percent of these plans offer some sort of match—the median being 3 percent and the average being 3.5 percent.

The way most of these 401(k) matches work is something like this: the company will match every dollar the employee contributes to their 401(k) up to, for example, 6 percent of their salary. So if the employee earns $100,000 and contributes 6 percent ($6,000) toward their 401(k), the company will do the same, resulting in $12,000 being deposited into the employee's 401(k). This is called a "dollar-for-dollar" match. The key here is that the employee has to contribute that amount; if they don't, the company won't either. This is why it's called a "company match"— the company is literally matching your money dollar for dollar. Now, some company matches will match a percentage of the employee's contribution rather than the whole amount—the employee has to contribute, let's say, 6 percent in order for the company to put in 3 percent. This is obviously a lower match than dollar-for-dollar, *but it's still free money!*

And saving for retirement is something you should be doing anyway! It's so important that Congress just passed

7 G. E. Miller, "Does Your 401K Match Up Against the Averages?," 20somethingfinance, last modified November 3, 2023, https://20somethingfinance.com/401k-match/#:~:text=According%20to%20the%20Bureau%20of,sad%20statistic%20in%20itself)%3A.

a bipartisan legislative bill (the SECURE Act 2.0) that would automatically enroll those who are eligible into retirement accounts when they first start working at a company. In other words, the next job you get, you might be automatically enrolled in their retirement account! (You should double-check either way, though.)

Of course, 3 percent or 6 percent might be all you feel you can afford to save, which is definitely better than nothing, but if you can, you should be investing at least 20 percent of your income (before taxes). Anything additional will just improve "future you's" finances. "Future you" will thank you.

PART TWO: ESPP

Companies want their employees to be invested in them. It makes sense that the more an employee is invested in the company they work for, the more they want to see the company succeed. And who better to make a company succeed than its employees? This is a huge reason companies offer employee stock purchase plans (or ESPP for short). I'll give a common real-life example I've encountered in my career to help you better understand how this works and why it's such a good deal. Your situation may be different, so talk to a financial advisor or otherwise educate yourself to ensure that you truly understand your specific situation.

In this example, the company that provided an ESPP would allow you to invest up to 10 percent of your salary toward the plan. The company would allow you to purchase company stock directly at a 15 percent discount—either at the beginning or at the end of a six-month period, whichever was cheaper. Read that a few times and let it sink in. Still don't follow? For instance, if the stock at the beginning of the six months is worth $100 per share and at the end of the six months is worth $115 per share, the employee pays only $85 per share at the end of the six months. I'll repeat that. The employee pays $85 for a share that's now worth $115. You know what that $30 difference is called? FREE MONEY!

I know what you're thinking: "But what if the stock goes down during those six months? Is it still a good idea to participate?" Absolutely! Let's pretend the opposite happened and the company stock went from $100 down to $85 during those same six months. Remember that you the employee get a discount of 15 percent off the beginning or end of the six months, whichever is lower—$100 and $85, in this case. In this scenario, you would have paid $72.25 per share for a stock that is now worth $85. That $12.75 is what again? FREE MONEY!

There is one small thing to keep in mind: you shouldn't cash out this stock for at least one year in most cases, because you'll have to pay income tax on the gains for that free money. It might be different depending on where you live or your specific situation, so I suggest looking into it for yourself (talk to a financial advisor or accountant, or google it). Once that year is past, you may want to sell quickly and diversify your investment to reduce risk. If you don't sell and the company goes bankrupt, you may lose all your money—or the company might skyrocket, and you could make a ton of money. It's really up to you if you want to take on that risk. Either way, the taxes likely only apply to that free money, so it's almost always a no-brainer to participate.

PART THREE: PROFIT SHARING

Remember how I said companies want their employees invested in them? Another way companies nudge their workers to invest is by distributing some of their proceeds among the employees via what's called *profit sharing*. The business has some formula to calculate how much profit it gives to its employees, often in the form of a bonus check or company stock. I'll give an example of a time that I worked for a company that offered a profit-sharing 401(k)

plan. This program was almost too good to be true. And yes, there were people who *turned down this free money*.

The process at the company I worked for (which may not be the standard) was this: if you simply participated in the company's 401(k) plan (the minimum to participate was 2 percent of your salary), you were eligible for the profit sharing at the end of the year, with the profits paid toward your 401(k). Their profit sharing had averaged roughly a 14 percent payout since its inception. To put it another way, if you simply put 2 percent of your salary toward your 401(k)—and again, you should be saving more than that for retirement anyway—the company would, on average, deposit an additional 14 percent of your salary into your 401(k) at the end of the year. That's a 700 percent match, if you want to think of it that way!

The worst part? I knew a woman who'd worked there for more than thirty years. At her retirement party, she admitted that she had never participated in the profit-sharing 401(k) plan! She estimated that the money she'd missed out on would have easily been worth *several million dollars* by the time she retired—and she lost out on it simply because she wanted to take home an extra hundred bucks or so per paycheck.

PART FOUR: EDUCATIONAL EXPENSES

While I was at my first job out of college, my manager asked me where I saw myself in five years. I didn't know at the time, but I knew I enjoyed mentoring and developing those around me; I knew I loved making as much of an impact as possible; and I knew I was open-minded and made rational and logical decisions.

My manager suggested that I pursue a career in management myself and pointed out that the company would reimburse a portion of my college expenses if I went back to school. Over my career, almost every company I've worked for has been willing to pay either a portion or all of my continued education expenses. Again, there was no way I was going to pass this up, and, as suggested, I went for my master's in engineering management.

Not only are companies often willing to invest in your education, there are scholarships out there willing to do the same. Usually, all you have to do is write an essay, fill out some paperwork, and submit the application. You often can even reuse the same essay over and over to apply to different scholarships. I went to school with several students who were actually *earning money* by going to school because of all the scholarships they had.

WHEN FREE MONEY ISN'T AVAILABLE TO YOU

The previous sections' free money might not be available to you. For example, maybe you're self-employed or run a small business. Still, there's likely still free money available to you somewhere. For instance, because of COVID-19, the CARES Act was put in place to help out business owners during the pandemic. There were a number of changes that helped small businesses get some free money. If you had a Small Business Administration (SBA) loan, the government made payments toward it on your behalf for a certain amount of time. There was also the Paycheck Protection Program (PPP) and its associated loan forgiveness. Ultimately, you could take a loan to pay your employees, and if you met the PPP requirements, you could apply for forgiveness of that loan.

And while some pieces of assistance like those might be tied to specific causes and exist for limited periods of time, they're far from the only ones to exist. Maybe you want to start up a business. A quick Google search will provide you with federal grants, state grants, local grants, corporate grants, grants for women, grants for minorities, grants for veterans, grants for immigrants, grants for felons, and grants for pretty much any start-up company you can think of. There's always free money to be had—you just have to put in the effort to find it.

WHAT SHOULD YOU DO WITH ALL THIS FREE MONEY?

If you read the previous few lessons, you might be finding yourself with a ton of free money just burning a hole in your 401(k). But what should you do with it? *For the love of God, do not touch it!* I won't get into the details of it now, but if you cash out your 401(k) early, just know that you will likely be charged significant fees as well as having to count it as income for that year (which will likely result in your withdrawal being taxed at an *even higher* tax rate). Seriously, do not cash it out early. Just pretend it doesn't exist. Leave it for retirement so you won't have to eat cat food to survive. Unless you really want to eat cat food—in that case, more power to you.

CHAPTER 4:

SOME BASICS OF PERSONAL FINANCE

Most of this book covers the basics, but some of the following concepts, in my opinion, are the *foundations* of these basics. These are concepts that some people go through their entire lives without truly understanding—and are likely worse off because of it.

TAX BRACKETS

There's plenty of confusion when it comes to tax brackets. The most common thing I hear from people is "there's no point in making more money because it will bump me into the next tax bracket." These people's (incorrect) rationale is that if you break the imaginary tax bracket threshold, then *all* of your income is taxed at the increased tax bracket. This couldn't be more wrong. Even the richest of people are taxed the same rate as everyone else on the first dollars they earn. Only the money they earn *above* that threshold is taxed at the next bracket.

For this particular topic, let's simplify the existing tax bracket system (there are currently seven federal income tax brackets). Let's pretend there are only two tax brackets and the "threshold" is $50,000. In this example, anything less than $50,000 is taxed at 10 percent, and anything over is taxed at 20 percent. If you earn $49,999, you will be taxed $4,999.90. However, if you earn $50,001, you will be taxed $5,000.20—a difference of $0.30 on those two dollars. One dollar is taxed at 10 percent, and the next dollar is taxed at 20 percent.

Again, even the richest of people who have the majority of their money taxed in the highest tax brackets also have their first dollars taxed at the lowest bracket. Whether you earned $50,000 or $1 billion in the previous example, the first $50,000 is *always* taxed at 10 percent. To summarize, when it comes to tax brackets, you should *not* be choosing to earn less in an attempt to be taxed less. That just isn't how tax brackets work. This doesn't mean you can't reduce your tax burden, however, and one great way to pay less in taxes is by *flattening out your income*.

FLATTENING OUT YOUR INCOME

When it comes to your retirement account, a key to reducing your taxes is to flatten taxable income year over year. Assume that you earn $1 million over the course of your lifetime and live to be one hundred years old. To simplify this example, pretend the government only taxes at two rates: 10 percent up to $50,000 and 50 percent for anything over that. (In real life, there are many more "tax brackets" than this, but they increase as you earn more just like our example does.)

For the first scenario, let's take it to the extreme and pretend we've earned 100 percent of our income in one year. In other words, we earned $1 million the first year we worked and will earn nothing after that until we die. In the year we earn this $1 million, the first $50,000 is taxed at 10

percent, so we're taxed $5,000 on this $50,000. Awesome! But uh-oh—the remaining $950,000 is taxed at 50 percent, resulting in $475,000 in taxes. To calculate the total tax on that $1 million, we add the $5,000 from the initial $50,000 to the $475,000 we were taxed on the remaining $950,000 and get a grand total of $480,000 in taxes, which brings our net profit (what actually goes into our bank account after taxes are paid) to $520,000.

For the second scenario, let's pretend that we earn a "flattened-out" income during our working career. Let's pretend we work for fifty years in total—which isn't completely unrealistic. Divide $1 million by fifty years, and it comes out to $20,000 per year. Anything below $50,000 in one year is taxed at 10 percent. Since we never break $50,000, everything we earn every year is only taxed at 10 percent! Total tax throughout our lifetime? $100,000. Net profit? $900,000. We reduced our tax burden from $480,000 to $100,000 just by flattening out our income!

So, how can you use the strategy of flattening out your income to save on taxes? We'll talk about this more during the next chapter on types of investments. For now, just remember what you've learned about tax brackets and the principle of flattening your income.

COMPOUND EARNINGS AND THE RULE OF 72

The previous illustration shows a simple graph displaying *exponential growth*. For this example, pretend you consistently earn the S&P 500's average return of roughly 10 percent. Initially, you invest $1,000, earning a 10 percent return per year thereafter. In your first year of accumulating interest, you earn $100, for a grand total investment of $1,100. The second year, you earn $110, for a total of $1,210. Notice that this is more than the previous year, and you didn't invest anything additional. The next year, you earn $121, for a total of $1,331. Again, you earned more than the previous year without any additional investment. This is what's called *compound earnings*. Without investing anything additional, your investment should grow *exponentially*. Every year you leave your money invested, it grows by even more than it did the years prior.

To build off this example, if you invest $1,000 per month, work for forty years, and earn a 10 percent return during each of those forty years, you'll have roughly *$6.46 million* when you retire. If you instead decide to wait until your thirtieth year of work to begin investing, you'll need to invest about *$31,500 per month* to have the same amount at retirement. You can clearly see in this example why investing early and letting your money grow for as long as possible is so important. To simplify the lesson to be learned here, (1) begin investing as early as possible, even if it's only a small amount, and (2) don't cash out for as long as possible.

The "Rule of 72" is just a simple way to estimate how long it will take to double your money. To calculate it, you divide 72 by the rate of return to calculate how long it will take to double your money. In the previous example, we had a return of 10 percent annually. The basic math here is as follows: 72 / 10 = 7.2. In other words, our initial investment of $1,000 will take roughly 7.2 years to double. That means that our $1,000 investment becomes roughly $2,000 after 7.2 years. After roughly 14.4 years, it becomes $4,000. After roughly 21.6 years, it becomes $8,000, and so on. See how it's growing *exponentially*?

This is a great example of how compounding works. You earn money from the money you've earned—and the cycle continues until you cash out. Now you see that when you spend a little today instead of investing it, it is likely costing "future you" many times more than the sticker price.

THE 4 PERCENT RULE

Disclaimer: This rule is somewhat controversial. This is mostly because critics claim that it's not safe enough (or is too safe), that you'll likely need much more than this to survive, and so on. We'll address this in a second.

All right—so what is the "4 Percent Rule"? Depending on who you ask, you might get different answers. But to put it simply (and in my own words), the rule states that if you can live off 4 percent of your savings, then you can likely retire. The thought is that you can take out 4 percent in your initial year of retirement, then do the same in the years to follow (while also adjusting for inflation). So, if you have $1 million saved and you can live off an annual amount of $40,000 (4 percent of $1 million), you can likely retire.

Now, I think this is oversimplifying things a bit, but my opinion is that most people don't have anywhere near enough to retire anyway, so who cares? If you aren't fiscally responsible, your money likely won't last you through retirement no matter what. And if you are fiscally responsible, you likely will cut back to try to make *sure* your money will last you through retirement no matter what (including a buffer for "unexpected" expenses). It is obviously easier to live off more money than less money, *so you should save as much as you possibly can before you retire.*

INFLATION

If you invest in "low-risk investments," your money probably isn't making as much for you as it could. Actually, you're probably losing more than you're earning due to inflation. Let's say the average inflation over the course of your life is an annual rate of 3 percent. Let's also say that you invested in one of the lowest-risk investments there is:

your own savings account. You researched many savings accounts and came upon one that provides an "excellent" return of a whopping 1 percent (yes, 1 percent is actually pretty high for a savings account). These numbers aren't too far off—go research it yourself if you don't believe me.

What this means is that your money is worth about 2 percent less every year. Doesn't seem too bad, right? But over the course of your life, that 2 percent becomes a much bigger deal. Pretend we put $100,000 into our savings account when we're thirty years old. By age sixty, that $100,000 is now worth an equivalent of just under $55,000. Because you played it safe, you lost over $45,000 of your money's initial worth. Instead, let's pretend you put that money into the S&P 500, which underperformed its historical average and only gave an annual return of 7 percent. Adjusting for the 3 percent inflation, your money grows at a rate of 4 percent. That $100,000 is now worth over $324,000. Would you rather have $324,000 or $55,000 when you take it out at sixty?

Now, pretend the S&P 500 outperformed its historical average by about the same amount—let's say that the annual return is 13 percent (or a growth rate of 10 percent if you factor in the 3 percent inflation). That $100,000 will be worth about $1.75 million in present value. Would you rather have $1.75 million or $55,000? In my opinion, it's a no-brainer; the risk is worth the reward.

Of course, savings accounts and other low-risk investments have their (limited) place. We'll talk more about that in the next chapter.

FUTURE VALUE OF MONEY CALCULATORS

While in my master's program, I learned some financial concepts, such as the time value of money (TVM) and how to calculate your money's future value (FV). Fortunately, you can skip all the boring stuff that comes with a master's degree. Instead, just google "future value of money calculator," click on a (trustworthy) site, and try out the previous section's example for yourself. Enter the numbers that I mentioned earlier in this chapter: $100,000 with a return rate of -2 percent (1 percent return from your savings account minus 3 percent for inflation). Put down a time period of thirty years, and you should get roughly the same results I said you would. Now do the same thing with a return of 10 percent. See the difference? Try changing the amount of time to ten years, twenty, forty, and so on.

As you can see, the longer you keep your money invested, the more money you'll likely end up with in the long run. This is obviously why you should wait as long as possible before cashing out your investments. The same goes for the interest rate. The more you can increase your rate of return, the more you will see dramatic increases in the amount you have when you take it out. A simple fee of 2 percent might not seem like a lot, but it dramatically decreases how much you'll have in twenty, thirty, or forty years. Try subtracting 2 percent from the interest and see what you end up with in that calculator.

Personally, I love playing with FV calculators. I love changing around numbers and seeing how they will impact me in the future. I love planning out retirement at different ages and watching how much it changes my financial future. It makes the prospect more real and provides some motivation to stay the course.

FINANCIAL ADVISORS

To simplify things a bit, there are generally three kinds of financial advisors: commission-based, fee-based, and fee-only financial advisors. In my opinion, the main difference between these types of financial advisors is how they are paid. Most financial advisors provide you with a service, such as their expertise and advice. Some financial advisors also are able to offer you their products, such as investments or insurance. Let's go through these types of financial advisors so you can see the differences between them.

Commission-Based

My experience with commission-based financial advisors has been very similar to my experience with commission-based car salespeople. The moment they see you, they run over to you and don't let you out of their sight. They hound you and make you feel stupid for not buying their product without hesitation. A key difference here is that I've never had a car salesperson show up on my front doorstep even after I ask them to go away (yes, I've had financial advisors stop by my house even after I asked them to leave me alone). They make money when you buy their product, so it's only natural that they want to make a sale. The question is, would you trust a car salesperson whose money depends on your purchase to simply go out and buy a car for you without your keeping a watchful eye over them? No? Then why would you trust a commission-based financial advisor to handle your entire life savings without keeping a very watchful eye over them?

Fee-Based

Fee-based financial advisors are probably better, right? Not so fast. Fee-based advisors are very similar to those who work on commission. They might collect commission on what they're selling you, they might charge you a fee for giving you advice, or they might do both. Not only do they charge you for buying their product (which they likely make money off of), but they also charge you for their advice to buy it from them! That's like a car salesperson who not only tries to get you to buy the car they're selling but charges you a fee simply for *telling* you that you should buy the car they're selling. How wonderful! Again, my personal opinion is to steer clear of anyone that is making money off what they're selling you—you just don't know whether they truly have your best interest in mind, or their own.

Fee-Only

The last type of financial advisor uses a fee-only model, which is exactly as it sounds. They only collect a fee for giving you advice. They serve as a third party, (hopefully) acting in your best interest. There shouldn't be a conflict of interest between the two of you because, well, they aren't (or at least shouldn't be) making money off your purchases. Not only do they not collect commission, they probably won't even try to sell you anything, because they likely have nothing to sell. Yes, they could tell you to go buy something from some company, but since you know they won't be making money off that transaction, it's probably what they truly think is best for you. In my opinion, their lack of any conflicts of interest means the fee-only advisor is the best type of financial advisor. Often, if they do a good job, you refer the advisor to your friends, and they increase their clientele. That's how they make more money—by making their customers happy and, therefore, growing their customer base.

All that being said, I personally don't trust anyone when it comes to my hard-earned money—even if they have a legal obligation to have my best interest in mind (known in the industry as a *fiduciary duty*). In the past, I've met with financial advisors, taken their advice, educated myself on the topic and/or product they are suggesting (via a simple Google search), and made an educated decision based on the facts presented to me. I strongly suggest you do the same. Educate yourself—understand what your financial advisor is telling you and why they're saying what they're saying. Ask them to explain it so you truly feel comfortable with the situation. If you feel pressured, walk away. If you're lost when it comes to what's happening with your money, then you might as well be writing a blank check to a car salesperson.

THE MORE YOU EARN, THE MORE YOU CAN SAVE

When you earn more, you spend more. Almost everyone does it, myself included. Picture your current money situation. Now imagine yourself earning half as much. What would you change about your life? No more going out to eat? A cheap used car? A cheaper place to live? Or maybe you'd even have to move back in with your parents? Almost everyone has ways they could tighten their belt.

Now imagine yourself earning twice as much. What would you change? Would you buy that new car? A huge house? New, more expensive clothes? Would you go out to eat more often and at more expensive restaurants? As you increase your income, you naturally increase your expenses—but why?

Let's pretend you earn $50,000 annually and that your expenses take up $45,000 of that per year (we'll ignore taxes and other variables for this example). You're able to save $5,000 per year. Not bad. Now let's pretend you switch jobs and earn twice as much. Without thinking, you might expect that you can therefore save about twice as much, or $10,000, right? It makes sense. Your income doubled, so your savings rate doubled. This is very, very wrong. If you *choose* not to increase your expenses, you can now save roughly eleven times as much. Why? Your expenses didn't increase. In that example, you doubled your income, so you're now earning $100,000 annually. Your expenses are still $45,000, so you are able to save $55,000—eleven times your previous savings amount of $5,000.

This is why increasing your income matters so much—and why *not increasing your expenses* matters just as much. (Remember the net profit formula from earlier?) When most people earn more, they spend more. Why? Because they can—what a terrible reason. I understand it's somewhat unrealistic to keep your expenses the *exact same* as you earn more. I'm guilty of it. I lived off Maruchan ramen noodles and Jack's pizza while in college—I don't do that anymore. However, I do try to keep my expenses down as much as reasonably possible. Keep the net profit equation in mind anytime you are tempted to increase your expenses. Try your best to save extra income. It will be *pure net profit*.

CHAPTER 5:

EXPLORE THE TYPES OF INVESTING

There are times when you can make money through acts that involve little to no risk, such as writing a book or building and publishing an app. For this section, however, we'll be covering various types of good old-fashioned investing—which almost always includes some risk.

LOW-RISK SAVINGS OR INVESTMENTS

We talked about what happens if you put money into a savings account long term when we talked about inflation. When you compare that outcome with investing in the S&P 500, it might not be the best idea—but these low-risk investments do have their (limited) place. A basic example of this is when you're nearing retirement and simply don't want to take on as much risk anymore. In this case, you might want to move more and more of your money to low-risk, low-reward investments, such as high-yield savings accounts, treasury bonds, or certificates of deposit (CDs). Personally, I would put in only the amount that would help me sleep well at night and then leave the rest in stocks. But again, it's *your* decision regarding how much risk *you* are willing to take on.

The other (limited) place for having money in a savings account is what many call an "emergency fund" or "safety net." I save about three months' worth of expenses in case I were to lose my job or some other *emergency* were to occur. I don't touch this money or even think of it as being spendable in any way outside of this. It's purely meant as a buffer in case shit hits the fan. Again, how much you have in your savings really depends on your individual situation and how much risk you want to take on. Some people recommend three months' worth of expenses; others might recommend up to a year or more. It's ultimately up to you to decide. That being said, you should have some sort of backup so that you never have to touch your retirement accounts in case of emergency. That money is for retirement and nothing else.

ROTH VS. TRADITIONAL

I briefly mentioned IRAs and 401(k)s previously. But you also have a choice between *Roth* and *traditional* IRAs or 401(k)s. You need to understand how both work so you can decide which one will offer the best return on investment for your situation.

In general, when you hear "Roth," it just means that the money you're investing with is *after-tax* money—or money that the government has already collected tax on. I'll give an example: I earn $100 (before tax) and decide to put all of it into my *Roth* 401(k). Before it goes into my Roth 401(k), the government taxes it—let's pretend at 20 percent. What ends up in my Roth 401(k) is $80. What's nice about this is that when I cash out this money (as well as additional earnings it has accrued), I don't pay taxes on *any of it*. Continuing with this example, let's pretend that when I retire, I've doubled my money—I get to cash out $160 *tax-free*! It doesn't even count as income at the end of the year when I cash it out (because it already counted as income *the year that I invested it*).

Now, let's play out this same scenario had we put the money into a *traditional* 401(k). What's "traditional" mean? It means that you're investing *before-tax* money. In this example, I again earn $100 (before tax) and invest that $100 into my traditional 401(k). The government pretends I didn't even earn it for that year; it doesn't show up on my income taxes at the end of the year, and I see $100 in my traditional 401(k). Great! Retirement comes and I decide to cash it out. The money still doubled the same as in the previous example, so now I'm cashing out $200. For this example, let's pretend we're taxed at the exact same rate as the Roth example mentioned previously: 20 percent. After taxes, we end up taking home $160—the exact same as the Roth example!

That's right, folks. Do you remember the commutative property of multiplication you learned back in sixth grade? In other words, a × b = b × a. In this case, ($100 × 0.8) × 2 = ($100 × 2) × 0.8. In the end, you still end up with $160.

But wait—if we end up with the same amount of money, then what's the point? The point is that we skipped a key component of this example, one that we'll cover in the next lesson.

FLATTEN YOUR INCOME: REVISITED

Remember what we learned about flattening your income in the last chapter? This is why it matters.

To maybe oversimplify things, if you think you'll earn less now than in the future, you likely should invest in a Roth retirement account so that you get taxed less now versus more in the future. If the opposite is true (you're earning more now compared to the future), then you should do the opposite and invest in a traditional retirement account. To simplify things even further, if you're just starting out in your career, I'd definitely suggest going with a Roth. As you work more and more years—and earn more and more money every year—you may want to slowly transition over to a traditional retirement account. Obviously, this math isn't completely perfect and I've simplified things a lot, but it's close enough to *flatten out your income* quite a bit in the government's eyes. We'll dive more into this in a second.

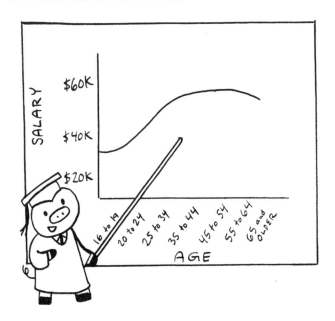

The previous graph shows the rough curve of a typical person's earnings by age at the time of this writing. For the example that follows, let's pretend you earn exactly what's listed in this graph throughout your lifetime. For this example, let's ignore inflation and pretend tax laws don't change at all in your lifetime. When you are new to the workforce, you earn less relative to when you've worked for many years. Once in retirement, you now are living off your investments; your overall income (the money you saved before tax, Social Security, and/or pension) goes down a bit compared to when you were earning a paycheck, and you are no longer contributing to your retirement.

Let's walk through two situations (again, with the numbers in the graph). In the first one, you are new to the workforce. In this situation, you earn less than "future you." You want to maximize what the government taxes as income now because you're currently being taxed only in the lower tax brackets. In other words, you probably will want to invest in a Roth 401(k) and/or Roth IRA so that you pay taxes now. Then, when you take the money out in retirement, it won't matter that you're earning relatively more because the amount taken from your Roth retirement account will be completely tax-free. Not only that, but this small amount you saved will likely be worth a whole lot more due to compound earnings over the many years it was invested.

In the next situation, you've worked for a while or maybe are even nearing retirement. You've steadily increased your income over the years so that you're making more now than when you first entered the workforce. When you retire, however, you might be expecting that your income will decrease. In other words, this stage of your career is likely the time when you're earning the most and would be paying the most in taxes if the government were to tax it now. In this situation, you want to reduce what the government taxes and should likely invest in a traditional retirement account. This way, you won't pay taxes now and will instead delay them until you're earning less during retirement.

I skipped a lot of the details and have flattened things into an easily digestible explanation, but this really is the core of how Roth and traditional retirement accounts can be used to your advantage—and save you a lot of money in the long run! Understand how to flatten out your income in the government's eyes, and you're probably in pretty good shape.

BROKERAGE ACCOUNTS AND THE STOCK MARKET

When you invest in stocks through a brokerage account, you're investing with after-tax money. So it should be similar to a Roth retirement account when it comes to taxes, right? Not at all. If you recall, the nice thing about a Roth IRA or Roth 401(k) is that you pay taxes up front and *never pay taxes on that account again*—even the money you earn. When you invest in the stock market through a brokerage account, however, it might be after-tax money, but you'll be taxed *again* on the gains (or what you earned). So if you invest a dollar in stocks and wait forty years, that dollar might now be worth $100—and you'll have to pay taxes *again* on the $99 you earned, which is almost the entire amount! When you compare that to the Roth IRA or Roth 401(k), you can obviously see why it's so advantageous to invest in your retirement accounts before investing in the stock market via a brokerage account—you don't end up paying taxes twice!

Let's say that you have $100 extra after maxing out your 401(k) and IRA (there are limits to how much you can put into each of them) and decide to invest it in the stock market. Your investment doubles in a month! Wow! What should you do with it? Don't touch it quite yet. If you cash out that $200, you now have to pay income tax on what you made, called "*short-term* capital gains tax." The key here is to let it sit long enough until you only have to pay what's known as "*long-term* capital gains tax." The time period you need to wait from the initial investment is, at the time of this writing, one year. If you let your money sit for more than that year, you'll likely only have to pay somewhere between 0 and 20 percent, depending on your tax bracket for that year. This is why it's most likely advantageous to always keep your stocks for *at least* a year. Again, I suggest buying stocks and immediately trying to forget that you even bought them. If you want to invest in something else, use your next paychecks to invest in it rather than selling old stock to invest in new stock. For all the reasons I've explained up until this point, my general rule for myself is to simply *not sell or cash anything out until retirement. Period.*

Another double-edged sword when it comes to brokerage accounts is that they're relatively easy to get to. You can likely cash out a brokerage account in a matter of a week or so. I don't like to have money sitting in a savings account. It isn't earning money for me there, and it's also too easy to get to when I have the urge to buy something stupid. And as previously mentioned, due to inflation, you're likely losing money by having it sit in a savings account. With a brokerage account, my money is invested in the S&P 500 or various companies that I believe in, which, on average, is making me significantly more money than a savings account would. In case of a true emergency (I mean a really, really, *really* big emergency), I can cash some of it out—and, yes, pay taxes on what I earned. I have yet to run into a true emergency where I've needed to cash any money out of my brokerage account, though.

To quickly recap: I put money into my brokerage account after maxing out all my retirement vessels—401(k), IRA, HSA, and so on—and I still treat it similarly to my retirement vessels. Deep down, I know that if I run into an *extreme* emergency, I would take that money out before I would ever consider touching a retirement account.

WHAT SHOULD YOU INVEST IN?

I've heard people say they don't invest in stocks simply because they don't know what to invest in. If you don't know which stocks are going to make you money, then you are in the same boat as literally everyone else on the planet, except for insider traders (look up what Martha Stewart went to jail for if you don't know what *insider trading* is).

So if you don't know what to invest in and you can't insider trade (because you *shouldn't* insider trade), what should you invest in? Regarding my personal brokerage account—not my 401(k)—I'm a fan of investing money in places you personally care about. If you care about animals, google "stocks that help animals" and invest in those. If you care about the environment, google "stocks

that help the environment." Not only will you probably make money, you'll also be helping those companies accomplish something you care about.

Two major options you have for investments beyond individual stocks are the S&P 500 and hedge funds. I won't get into the details, but put simply, the S&P 500 can be thought of as a stock index that combines the stock of the roughly five hundred largest US companies into a single stock index. Many consider its performance a good representation of how the entire US stock market is doing. Hedge funds, on the other hand, are essentially funds run by people trying to maximize profits by researching and guessing what will perform best. They might be constantly changing investments behind the scenes if they think one stock will do well today and another will do well tomorrow.

There are many people and companies invested in the S&P 500, reducing the cost of investing in it to a fraction of most hedge funds'. Since it's invested in so many companies, the S&P 500 is already well diversified. This is why I, personally, put all my 401(k) money toward it and plan to continue to do so going forward.

There are people out there much smarter than I am when it comes to investing, however. Warren Buffett is one of those people. He's made a fortune for himself and has proven himself to be incredibly wise when it comes to investing time and time again. He once issued a challenge wagering $1 million of his money that a hedge fund couldn't stand up to an S&P 500 index fund over the following ten years. A (naïve, in my opinion) company took the bet. Warren Buffett won the wager outright, with the S&P 500 completely dominating the challenge. You see, most index funds that follow the S&P 500 have extremely low fees when compared to most hedge funds while still providing a hefty return (over 10 percent annually since the S&P 500's inception at the time of this writing).

In a financial course in grad school, I learned that people act irrationally, illogically, and, most important, unpredictably. This is exactly what hedge funds try to do—predict the unpredictable—and is likely just one more reason Warren Buffett won the bet. It costs money to have people trying to predict what's going to happen, often with little to no success. This is where the S&P 500 succeeds.

Yes, the S&P 500 is still "risky"—or at least more unpredictable than letting money sit in your savings account, a treasury bond, or a CD. If you recall, however, the S&P 500 has averaged an annual return of over 10 percent at the time of this writing. There is simply no treasury bond or CD that can come anywhere near that rate of return. If you're young and able to ride out the ups and downs over the long run, you have a great chance of coming out very, very far ahead by the time you retire. Also, investing in the S&P 500 helps out those companies and the US economy, which will also positively impact the value of your money down the line.

Don't trust me, though; look into it for yourself. Keep a close eye on any fees you are being charged by investing in an index fund, a hedge fund, or any other investment; then make your own decisions. Your situation likely differs from mine; maybe you're nearing retirement and stocks are too risky to put all your money toward. Again, I'd suggest finding a fee-only financial advisor whom you trust to review your personal situation with you. Look into and understand the advice they are giving, and then make your own decisions.

THE STOCK MARKET IS SCARY

The stock market is scary. When it's going down, it seems like it will go down forever. Your hard-earned money is slowly, unbearably dwindling away, so you cut your losses and cash it out. In my opinion, this is the main reason the rich get richer while the poor get poorer (by "poor," I mean relative to the rich). The rich don't stop investing. They don't mind a little bump in the road. For the rest of us . . . well, this money might be our livelihood.

Let's give an example. Let's say that the average net worth of a "rich person" is $10 million. Let's say that the average net worth of an "average person" is $100,000. Both people invest 90 percent of their net worth into the S&P 500, and—uh-oh—it tanks, dropping 50 percent in a single day. To top it off, the rich person and the average person lose their jobs. It was a bad day.

To recap, the rich person invested $9 million and kept $1 million in their savings account, while the average person invested $90,000 and kept $10,000 in their savings account. The rich person, obviously, can last much longer without touching the money invested in stocks. The average person, however, is having a rough time. The average person runs out of money after three months and cashes out their 401(k), incurring penalties as well as income tax—ouch! Eventually, the stock market not only goes back up but breaks new records (as it has always done over and over throughout history); now the poor person has $45,000 (or less) to their name, while the rich person who never cashed anything out has, let's say, $15 million to their name. Do you see why the rich get richer while the rest of us are left in the dust?

My father always told me, "You won't win the lottery unless you spend a dollar." Statistically, it was terrible advice. When it comes to the stock market as a whole (or the S&P 500 in particular), history has shown that if you wait long enough, you'll win. Since the impact of the economy going down is much different for the rich versus the rest of us, the rest of us really do have to fight harder to not cash out when stocks go down. We have to fight the urge to sell when we hear someone ranting about how the sky is falling, or when the stock market actually *does* fall. If there's a lesson to be learned here, it's that you should do everything in your power to *not cash out* and leave that money in for truly as long as possible. I've already mentioned this, but I buy stocks and then pretend that investment no longer exists (until retirement, at least). If I want to invest in something else, I invest with future paychecks instead of selling and moving around money. This helps me with the urge to sell when someone yells that the sky is falling, because it's a personal rule of mine that I refuse to break.

HEALTH SAVINGS ACCOUNT (HSA): AN OFTEN-OVERLOOKED RETIREMENT ACCOUNT

A health savings account (HSA) is a savings account meant to encourage you to save for medical expenses and keep you from paying taxes for those same medical expenses. HSAs are only available to those with a high-deductible health insurance plan (HDHP) and are an attempt to help control rising health insurance costs. We won't get into how or why HSAs work, but we will review some of their tax advantages.

In general, HDHPs tend to be cheaper when compared to lower-deductible plans, allowing you to put that extra money toward an HSA. One nice thing about an HSA is that you can often invest this money similarly to how you would an IRA or brokerage account. If invested right and given enough time, your HSA will likely grow exponentially due to the miracle of compounding.

That said, my household doesn't even use our HSA money to pay for medical bills (yet). We pay for those out of pocket. We do this because we already max out all our other retirement accounts and still have some money left over. Here's an example: if we max out all our retirement accounts and then pay for medical bills with our HSA, we're paying with "tax-advantaged" dollars—or money that has a lot of tax advantages. So if you use this money for medical expenses, it never gets taxed. HSAs also allow you to invest this money, similarly to an IRA or 401(k). If you invest it, it likely will be worth significantly more in the future—and you can reimburse yourself at any point in the future for past medical expenses (as long as you had an HSA at the time of the medical expense). Or, you can use the money for medical expenses in the future and never have to pay tax on it. And if you don't want to use it for medical expenses at all, you can take it out for non-medical expenses once you turn sixty-five (at the time of this writing), paying income tax on it only when you take it out—just like a traditional 401(k) or traditional IRA! (However, if you want to just take the money out for non-medical expenses before you turn sixty-five, you'll be hit with income tax as well as a 20 percent penalty. Ouch. Don't do that.)

This is why my wife and I just pay for medical bills with excess after-tax money. If we invested it in a brokerage account (or bought stocks outside of a tax-advantaged retirement account), then we've already been taxed on it once (when we were paid), and we'll be taxed again on the profit it earns by the time we retire—and I assume almost all of it will be profit by that time due to the miracle of compounding. In other words, it's kind of like we're being taxed twice on that money! We don't want to do that. So we don't spend our HSA money. Instead, we save our medical receipts, and someday we'll reimburse ourselves with completely tax-free money.

Again, HSAs are only available to those with a high-deductible health insurance plan, which may or may not be right for you. You should do the math, guess as to whether or not you'll need to pay for medical bills that year, determine how much risk you're willing to take on (because you might be injured or the market could crash), and take other factors into consideration before choosing which medical plan is right for you. That said, we're fortunate enough to be able to afford a higher deductible *if* we were to get sick. My wife and I are both young and healthy overall, and, when doing the math, we felt that it made sense to go with a high-deductible health insurance plan and HSA.

DIVERSIFICATION

Now that you've taken the most important step and are saving and investing, you're probably wondering where the best place is to invest your money and how you should diversify to avoid too much risk. I've talked about this a little already, but there are many different strategies you might take. Personally, I'm a fan of Warren Buffett's advice and would never recommend against investing in the S&P 500 (or the number of stock tickers that track the S&P 500). It's already well diversified since it includes roughly the largest five hundred companies, has historically had great returns, and has fees that are typically close to nothing. Again, this is where I invest my entire 401(k).

With my IRA, HSA, and brokerage account money, I invest in companies that I think will succeed or will make the world a better place. Personally, I feel the companies most likely to succeed are those that prioritize customer-centricity. A quick Google search for companies with incredible customer-centricity will likely give you a rough list of companies that I've invested in. I also like to invest in companies that I think are improving the world in some way. But you don't have to do what I do; look into it for yourself and invest in companies that *you* believe in.

CHAPTER 6:

WHERE WILL YOU GO FROM HERE?

Assuming you aren't sixty-five and retired already, you probably have a little while until that time comes. Envision that future self. Close your eyes and picture that person's appearance, how they've aged, and what you think their finances might look like. How would you *like* their finances to look?

When you're aiming for the moon and you're slightly off, it's easy to make minor corrections early on, but it's a lot harder when you're flying past it. The same is true for retirement.

WE END UP WHERE OUR DECISIONS TAKE US

Without a strong financial mindset, we easily lose focus and give in to those purchases we don't really *need*. That being said, I'm a strong believer that most of us end up financially where our own decisions take us. Imagine that we hand a random person a large sum of money. Given enough time, they'd end up in the same financial spot as they would have without the extra money we handed them. Yes, there are exceptions, but there are also countless examples of this principle in action.

You've likely heard about professional athletes, musicians, actors, lottery winners, and so on who make fortunes through hard work or luck—and a few years, months, or even days after the money stops coming in, they're broke. Why is that? What it comes down to is that they don't know what to do with their money. They make poor investment decisions, spend as though the money fire hose will never stop, exist too much in the moment, and simply live beyond their means. If there's a lesson to be learned from these people, it's that no matter how much you make, you're only a few poor decisions away from being broke.

At the same time, there are those people you could drop in the middle of nowhere, with only the clothes on their back—and you'd still have to be nuts to bet against them. Would you really want to bet against someone like Warren Buffett, Steve Jobs, Bill Gates, Oprah Winfrey, or Mark Cuban? They've proven to make great investment decisions, work harder than almost anyone to guarantee their success, and never give up.

Regardless of your current financial situation, you are in control of your actions and decisions. You can always make decisions that lead to improvement over time.

JUST DO IT

To quote Desmond Tutu, "There is only one way to eat an elephant: a bite at a time." Saving enough to retire is definitely a very large task—especially when you're just starting. But you have to take that first step, stay motivated, and stay the course. Surround yourself with like-minded people. You might be surprised to find how many people out there are working toward the same financial goals you are. They probably include your closest friends and family. I've learned some of the most important financial lessons of my life from random conversations while visiting with someone close to me.

You also might be surprised to know how many people you've never heard of who have already made their fortunes simply by being frugal and making wise investment decisions that slowly moved them closer to a financial spot they wanted to be in. They stayed the course throughout their lifetime and likely worried little about money because of it.

If that's something you want, you just have to do it.

I'D LIKE TO LIVE AS A POOR MAN WITH LOTS OF MONEY.

—Attributed to Pablo Picasso